Holy Ground

Classic Arrangements of Power and Praise
for Solo Piano by Fred Bock

Contents

Fred Bock Music Company

HOLY GROUND

Geron Davis
Arranged by Fred Bock

With hushed awe (♩=92)

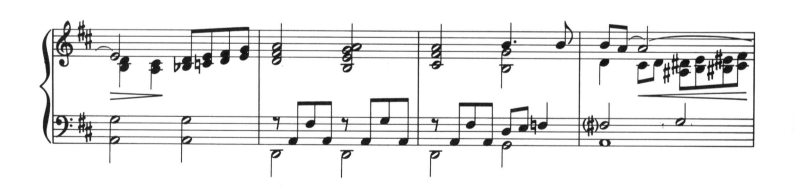

HOW MAJESTIC IS YOUR NAME

Michael W. Smith
Arranged by Fred Bock

PRAISE TO THE LORD, THE ALMIGHTY

LOBE DEN HERREN
Arranged by Fred Bock

JOYFUL, JOYFUL, WE ADORE THEE

Ludwig van Beethoven
Arranged by Fred Bock

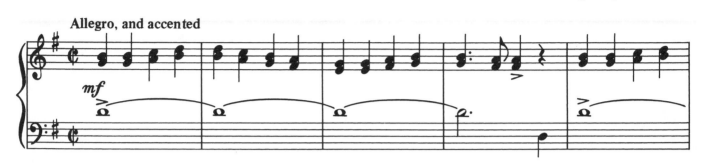

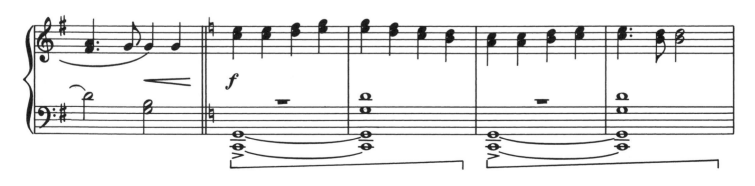

13

HALLE, HALLE, HALLE

Traditional Caribbean
Arranged by Fred Bock

With strength and majesty (♩ =100)

ff

* " Hallelujah Chorus"

Bright and happy

mf

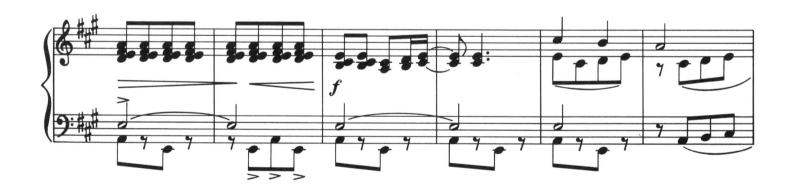

PRAISE THE NAME OF JESUS

Roy Hicks, Jr.
Arranged by Fred Bock

HOW BEAUTIFUL

Twila Paris
Arranged by Fred Bock

Warmly and tenderly

Like a hymn-Legato

HOLY, HOLY, HOLY

John B. Dykes
Arranged by Fred Bock

Majestically, with strength

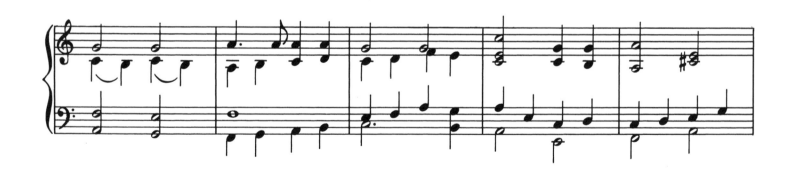

8 ba

THOU ART WORTHY

Pauline Michael Mills
Arranged by Fred Bock

HE IS EXALTED

Twila Paris
Arranged by Fred Bock

With exuberance and rhythmic drive

CREATIVE KEYBOARD COLLECTIONS

Piano by Fred Bock

FRED BOCK PIANO FAVORITES FOR EASTER BG0951 HL00310364
The first in the *Fred Bock Piano Favorites Series.* Includes settings for Palm Sunday and Holy Week ~
Because He Lives, The Easter Song, The Old Rugged Cross, We Shall Behold Him, Were You There? and seven
others. $10.95

BOCK'S BEST #1 . . . . BG0557 HL08738352
Fifty arrangements of hymns, gospel songs, and folk-hymns, including Fred Bock's famous setting of
Jesus Loves Me woven around Debussy's *Clair de Lune.* $24.95

BOCK'S BEST #2 . . . . BG0572 HL08738353
Fifty hymns and gospel songs ~ more of Fred's harmonically-rich style of piano writing. This
collection includes *My Tribute, A Mighty Fortress Is Our God, Easter Song, We Shall Behold Him, The Old
Rugged Cross,* and 45 more. $24.95

BOCK'S BEST #3 *FOR CHRISTMAS* BG0679 HL08738356
Twenty-five tremendous Christmas piano solos. All your favorites are here, *Silent Night, Go Tell It On
The Mountain, O Little Town of Bethlehem, Away In A Manger,* and many others, dressed up for the
holidays in their best Fred Bock arrangements. $12.95

BOCK'S BEST #4 . . . . BG0880 HL08738370
Fifty piano solos featuring Fred Bock's unusual and rich harmonic progressions. You will enjoy playing
these for offertories, preludes, or just for at-the-piano fun. Includes *We Will Glorify, It Is Well With My
Soul, Another Time, Another Place, How Majestic Is Your Name, The Wedding Song, I Love You, Lord,
People Need The Lord, Soon and Very Soon, Give Thanks,* and 41 more excellent titles. $24.95

BOCK'S BEST #5 . . . . BG0941 HL08738374
This consummate compilation of creative skill is crafted together to create a delightful composite of both
present and past. Choruses, contemporary titles, and classical choral works are combined with beautiful
arrangements of favorite hymns, all in the unique harmonic style of Fred Bock. Includes these new
arrangements, *Here I Am, Lord, Holy Ground, I Walked Today Where Jesus Walked, I Wonder As I Wander,
Jesus, Name Above All Names, The Lord's Prayer, The Majesty and Glory of Your Name, On Eagles' Wings,*
among the 50 total selections. $24.95

Piano Praise & Worship by Fred Bock

*Three invaluable volumes of innovative and inspirational arrangements of the most popular praise
and worship choruses. Challenging yet accessible, Fred Bock's settings of these favorite melodies are
especially appropriate for preludes, postludes and offertories.*

PIANO PRAISE AND WORSHIP BG0749 HL08738359
Includes *Majesty, O How He Loves You and Me, I Love You Lord, Thou Art Worthy, Give Thanks, How
Majestic Is Your Name, He Is Exalted,* among 8 others. $10.95

PIANO PRAISE AND WORSHIP #2 . . . . BG0788 HL08738361
All new arrangements, not appearing in any other Fred Bock collections, including, *Emmanuel, Jesus
Name Above All Names, This Is The Day, As The Deer,* plus 11 more. $10.95

PIANO PRAISE AND WORSHIP #3 . . . . BG0950 HL08738375
Fifteen new arrangements, including *Lord, I Lift Your Name on High, Spirit Song, Thy Word, My Desire,
Change My Heart, O God,* and *I Love the Lord.* $10.95

See following page for a listing of Praise & Worship collections for Organ and Organ-Piano Duets by Fred Bock.

Exclusively distributed by Hal Leonard Corporation
Available from your local music retailer

CREATIVE KEYBOARD COLLECTIONS

Piano and Organ Duets by Fred Bock

BOCK TO BOCK #1 . . . . BG0621 HL08738411

From a wonderful series of five volumes, this first collection features ten hymns specifically arranged for piano-organ duets. Titles include *And Can It Be, Love Was When, Moment By Moment, Near The Cross*, and more. Two copies are needed for performance. $10.95

BOCK TO BOCK #2 . . . . BG0686 HL08738412

The second volume of gospel greats for piano-organ duets features *My Tribute, Day By Day, Through It All, Ivory Palaces, Thou Art Worthy* and more. Two copies are needed for performance. $10.95

BOCK TO BOCK #3 . . . . BG0793 HL08738414

Fred Bock has again done a brilliant job arranging some of the most powerful contemporary Christian songs of today for piano-organ duets. Titles include *I've Just Seen Jesus, Great Is The Lord, How Majestic Is Your Name, In This Very Room, Majesty* and others. Two copies are needed for performance. $10.95

BOCK TO BOCK #4 *FOR CHRISTMAS* BG0821 HL08738415

Wonderful arrangements of several traditional and best-loved carols are housed in this collection for Christmas piano-organ duets, including *Away In a Manger, Joy To The World, There's a Song In the Air, Silent Night*, and others. Two copies are needed for performance. $10.95

BOCK TO BOCK #5 . . . . BG0909 HL08738417

Fred Bock concluded his organ and piano duet series with a fine cross-section of traditional hymnody and contemporary gospel songs. Titles include *Because He Lives, The Lord's Prayer, Lift High the Cross, Only Believe, Give Thanks, God of Grace and God of Glory* and more. Two copies are needed for performance. $10.95

SUNDAY MORNING WORSHIP BG0852 HL08738416

A collection of piano-organ duets, in the stylistic bravado of Fred Bock, includes majestic hymns *(Crown Him With Many Crowns, And Can It Be?, Joyful, Joyful We Adore Thee*, among others) as well as a popular Christmas title, *Angels We Have Heard on High*. Usable for the entire year. Two copies are needed for performance. $10.95

Organ and Piano Praise & Worship by Fred Bock

You asked for it, you got it! In Fred Bock's inimitable style of rich, lush harmonies, exciting rhythms, and tasty melodic intertwining, favorite praise and worship choruses are set in challenging and meaty arrangements for the experienced pianist and organist.

ORGAN-PIANO DUETS PRAISE AND WORSHIP *MEDLEYS* BG0757 HL08738413

An organ-piano duet collection of medleys of favorite praise songs, familiar hymns and gospel melodies. Four medleys of "Glorious, Majestic, Triumphant and Resplendent Praise" include *His Name Is Wonderful, He Is Exalted, To God Be The Glory, O For A Thousand Tongues To Sing, Holy, Holy, Holy* and many more. Two copies are needed for performance. $10.95

ORGAN PRAISE AND WORSHIP BG0923 HL08738404

Seven of the most popular of all praise and worship songs made entirely new by Fred Bock in this collection for organ. These are not typical hymn or gospel song settings; every one is a through-composed piece of music based on a praise and worship tune. Selections include *He Is Exalted, In My Life, Lord Be Glorified, We Will Glorify* and more. As Fred would say of this collection, *"This book will save your job!"* $10.95

See previous page for a listing of Praise & Worship collections for Piano by Fred Bock.